Songs

From My Soul

LARRY SMALLIE

Table of Contents

My Commitment i
Dedication: To Whom Should I Dedicate This Book? iii
Preface ix

Chapter 1: Soul Talk in the 1970s 1
    Words.. 2
    Trapped... 3
    Unseen 5
    What Will He Be 6
    Stand Up.. 9
    Lost.. 10
    Untouched 11
    In the Presence of My Enemies 12
    Procession 13
    Why... 14

Chapter 2: Soul Speak in the 1980s...................................17
    My Favorite Guy.. 18
    My Child 19
    Sunday in the Pasture.. 21
    Illuminus Light... 22
    Left You There.. 23
    Finding My Way 26

Chapter 3: Soul Words in the 1990s...................................31
    I Know You Are Here 32
    Of Her Love 34
    His Expression.. 36
    An Empty World... 37

The Illusion 39

Whispers 42

Pictures 44

Your Prison 46

The Dunes 48

Finding the Way 49

Another World 52

Win Your Heart 54

Now I Understand 56

Of Our Children 58

You Are My Sons 60

Ethan **62**

Little Man 63

Gwyneth **64**

Her Name 65

Chapter 4: Soul Whispers in the 2000s **67**

Loving Hearts 68

Glimpses 69

Her Eyes 70

Life Again 73

Our Love 74

Heartland 75

Let Me 78

I See You 79

I Know You 82

A Thinking Heart 83

The Dance 85

A Brighter Day 88

She Called 90

Who Is She 92

Touching You 94

I Will Fly 96

Images 99

Your Love.. 102

Since You 104

Reflections in Monterey.................................... 105

Two Hearts 108

Cleansed.. 110

On That Day.. 111

Chapter 5: Soul Music **115**

My First Song 116

The Child Left in Between................................. 119

Captured All My Love....................................... 122

Hear the Music 124

He's Always Been Here...................................... 127

It Couldn't Happen 130

Lost All the Light.. 132

Lucky in Love.. 134

Paradise... 136

Reflections 138

Seeing Her Seeing Me 140

Song in His Soul.. 143

Southern Lovin... 145

Wake Up and Listen 147

Welcome to My Dreams..................................... 150

Epilogue **152**

Forever 153

My Commitment

From the date "SONGS FROM MY SOUL" is available for purchase I will donate 100% of all profits/royalties for the first 6 months. Charities chosen will be for all children in need, sexually abused and physically abused children. And then for perpetuity I will continue to donate no less that 50 percent of all profits/royalties to these causes. It is my firm prayer that no child should suffer, but if they do we need to be there to for them in whatever way we can to support them in the healing.

I have personally known 5 people who have been the victims of childhood sexual abuse. I can honestly say I could almost see and feel the emotional wounds they suffered. For many, if not all, their scars remain in their lives today. The writing of my first book, SONGS FROM MY SOUL has been a gift from God as my soul began speaking to me the 1970s'. My hope and dream is that the proceeds from this book will in some way help to bring some healing to all children who have experienced any horrific abuse.

From 1969 through 1979 I was an elementary school teacher. In 2016 I reconnected with one of my former students via Facebook. She would now be in her forties. After exchanging a few private messages she texted me the following message:

"Mr. Smallie I know you could have not known that when I was in your fourth grade class I was sexually abused by my stepfather almost every day. Your class was the only safe place I had every week where you made learning fun. I will forever be grateful for that."

Thanks be to God that He created a safe place for this little girl. Perhaps, these words, verse and songs will create a similar safe place for those who read and experience them.

With loving gratitude,
Larry D. Smallie

Photograph by Nikki Harris

Dedication:
To Whom Should I
Dedicate This Book?

As I pondered this question the answer became relatively obvious as the title indicates, God gave me these songs/ pictures in words via my soul. Sometimes my soul would wake me and the middle of the night to write song lyrics on a piece of paper. At other times the whispering of my soul gave me free verse/poems to scribe. But my soul also gave many people on my journey here in this world who influenced and touched me in special and significant ways.

I find it imperative to start with two gifts in my life that cannot be measured. They are my sons, Todd Christopher and Brent Michael. They are precious to me beyond words as some of the free verse that came through my soul has been greatly influenced by my sons. One poem when my son Brent was just a child is entitled, "What Will He Be" another when Todd was a young adult, "Reflections In Monterey." There are many more embedded in the pages of what will be my first book.

Both my sons played guitar and bass. They attribute their interest in music to me as I taught myself to play acoustic guitar from an old Mel Bay guitar chord book in the early 60's. I played around my sons from the time they were toddlers. Songs from the 60's, 70's and 80's were heard over and over again in our home. In addition I took them to wedding ceremonies I used to play with an extremely gifted musician and a close friend with the voice of an angel. So my sons really had many strong musical influences. Yet I know the real gifts of music in how they play, hear, and absorb the sounds and rhythms came from God who speaks through their souls in this way as well.

Next are my parents Betty and Harvey. They gave me the gift of life as God had already planned them to be my parents. My dad always told the story of my mom putting me in their 1940 Ford Sedan as an infant and taking me to Third Baptist Church in our hometown. That was how she learned to drive a stick shift. She faithfully took me to that church all the way throughout my teenage years. She was a woman that truly lived and loved unconditionally. She started me on my spiritual journey early in life.

Some phycologists have stated that, "A father's love is earned and a mother's love is always given." This certainly was true in my experience as there was a time in my life when I felt that way. But eventually I came through a door of both understanding and forgiveness before he passed away. I realized that it was something he must have struggled all his life as well. My dad under all his gruff and toughness had a kind heart. He was very giving to many people during his lifetime. He loved his family and expressed it by working at 2 jobs a day sometimes. He gave my mother, two sisters and me a safe and secure home to live in and always provided for our needs.

Then there are my two sisters, Darla and Donna. We were born in 3 different decades. I was born in 1947, Darla in 1955 and Donna in 1960. Although there was a wide age difference we always have remained close and supportive of each other over the years. I have admired my sister Darla's ability to live through some tough relationship crises and become a very smart and strong independent women. She was transmuted the loving nurturing of our mother and the strong will of our father.

Big brothers always want to take care of their little sisters but my youngest sister Donna needed no taking care of. As the family story goes at elementary school in kindergarten she punched another little girl in the nose for looking over a bathroom stall at her. She inherited our dad's toughness and his giving heart underneath it.

Finally my cousin Dennis Edwards who became my first soulmate at the age of 10. God put us together for many reasons at that time in our lives and has continued to do so as we how both are approaching 70. Neither of us could probably explain why or how we are so connected. The closest explanation I can come is to what the research states about twins. Twins communicate with each other sometimes not even speaking and at other times can restate what each other may be thinking. Mystery is the best word for Den and me.

❧ v ❧

The major deep influence that is predominantly recorded in the preface of this book is the indescribable influence my wife Stephanie's love had and has on me until this very day. When we met the gift of her incredible big heart started me writing free verse again. Her unending love brought the world of music back into my heart and soul.

I truly thank God for placing all these people in my life as all their gifts are immeasurable. And for so many loving reasons I want to pay it forward to so many who may have not been loved the ways we all deserve to be loved. When you read the first page of this book entitled, "My Commitment" you will understand.

$\mathscr{Preface}$

After forty years of hesitant inspiration I began putting together this collection of what I call free verse back in December of 2001. I typed it all on an old desktop computer and printed out the pages to give as a Christmas gift to Stephanie, who I was very much falling in love with. On June 19 of 2004 she became my wife, my sweetheart, my soulmate and truly my very best friend.

Here is what I said as I began to put that book together:

"This book I am beginning is inspired by Stephanie who awakened in me a passion that has been long forgotten or left behind so many times ago in this life and most likely in other lifetimes as well. Her love, her big heart, her tenderness has whispered to me to listen to what my soul speaks so forcefully and so beautifully.

I am at all times amazed and humbled by this inner voice. It is as if someone else has taken control of my pen and written down my mental pictures in words and songs that reside in my soul. For this I am eternally grateful and thankful. It is a healing experience for me and one I will never be able to fully understand."

I believe that our souls speak to each of us in many different ways. This mystery of life is worth living. It whispers to me to slow down and listen. These pictures in words are what I hope others can see, feel, and experience too.

These visions of the deeper meaning in life have been coming to me in some form since the 1970s'. I have never paid attention to them like I do now. This is a season in my life that I desire to last forever. We are all be blessed with God given gifts and riches that our soul has for each of us if we trust ourselves enough to listen.

So here I am in 2017, almost 40 years later, beginning to put together the free verse, the poems, the songs that my soul has whispered to me over all these years. It is an exciting adventure to revisit these inspired words and songs. I have decided, or I should say that voice that speaks to me, has entitled this book Songs From My Soul.

LARRY D. SMALLIE 3/15/2017

Chapter 1

///////////////////////////////

Soul Talk in the 1970s

The free verse that briefly came to me in the 1970s' was totally unexpected. In 1970 and in 1973 I was blessed with two sons. In 1979 I was ending a ten year elementary teaching job and beginning a new sales career in educational publishing. I was simply trying to earn a living for my family. I continued to play guitar and sing as it was a blessing to me. I was simply too busy with life to listen to that inner voice. I had no context then, for what my soul was trying to tell me. Today I am very thankful for what wonders my soul has spoken, from a place within and to share with hearts unknown.

Words

Meaningless words
tossed into motion
left to be consumed
for those who are hungry
or too tired to resist

Dreamless nights
and deafening days
silenced only by
our own resistance

Lifted for a time
into it an ethereal cloud
transformed
into a being
not yet recognized

10/06/1976

Trapped

You put me in a box
and left me
on the shelf
expecting me
to stay there

You bound me in chains
and left me
weighed down
with more than you thought
I could bare

Silly of you
to have thought
that was all there was of me
how insignificant you must
have thought I was

– 10/07/1976

Unseen

He wheeled himself
into the stadium
but the applause
was not for him
he didn't even stand
for the kickoff
some laughed
and some stared
not that
his presence
was that entertaining
it's just hard
not to notice
a young man
in a wheelchair

11/03/1976

What Will He Be

What will he be
my son of four
all caught up
in his fantasyland

What will he be
the child adore
flying his ship
too unknown lands

As time goes on
will he travel far
from galaxies
to a falling star

Sometimes when I feel
he's so far away
he comes to me and
I hear him say

Daddy will we die
when we get old
daddy why don't I do
what I am told

At times like these
he touches me so
my heart reaches out
for words I don't know

Son, daddy loves you
is my only reply
daddy will be here
he won't die

So let's play a game
I'll let you choose
these precious moments
I will never lose

7/21/1977

7

Stand Up

Lay back in your chair old man
what peace do you find there
rocking away the hours you have left
for they probably will be few

Lay back in your chair old man
where others cannot touch you
your hope and passion for life diminished
and you only wait for night to come

The loves you have are all gone
and you search for no others
any hope for new beginnings
are all lost in old endings

Stand up from your chair, old man
and tell others of the life you've lived
show others you're hopes for tomorrow
or their lives may quietly fade away too

5/06/1978

Lost

I won't play these games
of life any longer
I've been captured
and rejected
left outside with
no invitation
to come in
I'm touched by things
I do not want
to be a part of
surrendered
secluded
silenced by
my own emotions
new freedom
has not found me

8/23/1978

Untouched

Some people never touch
the world I've touched
nor see the clouds like I
some people never sing my song
or ask the question why
you can't change it
some would say
why do you even try
what makes you think
you're better than me
the man who doesn't cry

5/11/1978

In the Presence of My Enemies

Come on
kick the ball
get him
can't you run
I've never seen
anything so stupid
God he's so lazy
this is his last game
don't let him
get by you
what an ignorant call

11/13/1978

Procession

Lights beaming
flags flapping in the breeze
creeping ever so slowly
seemingly and endless caravan
stopping for no one

– 7/10/1979

Why

He played the game well
learned the rules
suffered the injuries
paid the penalties
forgot the pain himself
when others refused
and with all he gave
he could not be declared
the winner

– 8/23/1979

Chapter 2

Soul Speak in the 1980s

During this decade I found myself lost in a world of confusion, doubt, personal challenges and choices. It was if in the midst of all the chaos and lack of confidence my soul began to speak even louder but less often. Looking back, it seems what was falling on deaf ears fell into my heart and soul to be awakened when I could hear more clearly and distinctly on another level. To me this is the miracle of soul speak, it waits for you.

My Favorite Guy

Sometimes the simplest words
are those words
which mean the most
words that make
you feel warm
feel wanted
feel loved
those words
often seem
hard to say
but when
your son says
you're my favorite guy
it touches
a very special
place in you
a place many
never touch
and a feeling
seldom realized

– 3/08/1984

My Child

My child lay
motionless
erased from time
time I did not
have to give
time that I did not
want to share

So I left him
lying alone,
helpless
wrapped up in blankets
I offered for security
for protection

As the years passed
there were times
he did not smile anymore
times when he only said hello

I wanted to
hold him
as I once had
to to capture a
moment
long forgotten
in each of us
a moment left only
in our reflections

– 2/11/1985

Sunday in the Pasture

The sacred cows lay
waiting on the banks
but their tongues were not soothed
their thirst was not quenched

They sought shelter in the shade
of a rapidly moving cloud
that passed as quickly
as did what little thoughts they had

Their desires were great
yet they settled for a
scratch against a Banyan tree
and a nap spent in collective solitude

Their travels seemed so worthy
of something more
yet they separated from one another
only to thirst and die
without understanding
why they ever came

– 04/21/1985

Illuminus Light

Let there be light
a light that
brings a new day
a day filled
with an
unending hope
a new person
a new desire
that awakens us
to our destiny

Left You There

I have left you
left you there
alone but not helpless
alone in your own world
a world marked with signs
signs that still must be interrupted
directions waiting to be followed
turns then must be made

You wait
sometimes not knowing
what you're waiting for
but still you wait
doors open
doors close
not to panic
there will be more
more than you may be willing
to accept at this place
in this time
more than you may be
willing to have

Yet it all still waits for you
with tenderness
with patience
so be kind to yourself
be loving to yourself
let the love expand
to embrace others
to hold their lives sacred
sacred as your own life is held

not in the balances of confusion
but held in the rooms of freedom
rooms that are infinite
spaces that are endless
places were only you can travel

– 5/1/1989

Finding My Way

Finding my way
through the fog
through the mist
traveling with caution
yet with trust
with hope
clearly where
I must go
where I am enticed to go
I must step slowly

As I let myself
slow down
my movements
become more natural
I can feel
a sense of peace
settle down into me
like a mist
it lays upon me
it penetrates into
my very being
it soothes my heart
refreshes my soul
it speaks softly
tenderly to me

Hush the mist says
hush and listen
to the silence
listen to the healing
the mist brings
listen to the voices
that come to
comfort you
to heal you
to bring to you
wholeness
where you can only
hear these voices
in the silence
in the midst
of this silence

So listen with
another ear
the ear of your heart
as the heart speaks
to your spirit
let that spirit
awaken your soul
so it may be healed
may be whole again

Let yourself rest
in the arms of Goddess
the Goddess who loves you
the Goddess who will
embrace the All of you
the All in you
the Whole which you
have not seen
She will show you
a new path
a bright light
a silent voice
that speaks of love
love that is infinite
that is unearned
that has no condition
except that of
coming home
to the place
you belong
that we all belong
in the arms
in the midst
of Her love

Photograph by Brent Smallie

So rest now and trust
that love that is
stronger than
any act
any reason
any belief
a force
a resonance where
no negativity can
stand against it
this love does not destroy
it transforms
it transmutes mere
man and woman
to their true essence
so let it begin

– 11/11/1989

Chapter 3

Soul Words in the 1990s

I had many awakenings and rebirths during this time. Many were unwanted, some were desired but most came from not seeing the world around me in ways that must have been intended. Once again my soul continued to speak more often and more clearly begging me to listen. When I did listen I ignored what I heard. Our negative ego takes us on a continuing path of self-direction rather than surrendering to that inner voice that takes us to our true spiritual home.

I Know You Are Here

In the silent language
that you speak
I know you are here
sometimes words
sometimes pictures
or maybe just a tap
on the shoulder
by someone unexpected

In the quiet images of the earth
I know you were here
as a speaker of the
magnificence of a sunset
or through the shadows
of the night
without a word
absent of sounds
paintings
void of pictures
still you come in
your silence to speak
beyond what words
can ever tell

– 4/28/1995

Of Her Love

I saw her
I felt her
I sensed her love
her love that
reached out
that enveloped
the one she loved

There was a peace
a stillness there
it rested upon them
like a ribbon of stardust
surrounding
embracing them
being held there
so very gently
in tenderness
tenderness that had
no words

They walked down
the corridor
embracing each other
and as they took each
small step
with each step
there was more light
more love
love radiated
throughout the space
they created

The light held the love
in all its majesty
and all its' realness
light and the love
were felt beyond
this place and
left its healing
a healing to be
touched again
held in each heart

– 1/17/1996

His Expression

I did not stop
this day
to write
to feel
to think
in a new way
as I reflect
it felt limiting
to not allow
this expression
of who I am
of what I know
of what I so strongly
desire to say
empty promises
are not for this
paper and pen
but truth has
a way of
seeping out
into the open
to be seen

– 4/02/1997

An Empty World

Emptiness
such emptiness
I see in the world
such emptiness
I feel in this world
and this world
is mine
the world I create
everyday

Sometimes I want to walk
to walk
walk into another world
a world full of hope
a world full of love
it seems I can
only stay a brief time
until I face my world
full of emptiness

How can something
full of emptiness
an emptiness that
moves from place
to place
an emptiness that
wants to be filled
a place where emptiness
is turned inside out
never to be filled

– 4/04/1998

The Illusion

It was hollow
so very hollow
illusion after illusion
trying to embrace me
trying to hold me
in place
as I struggled
the illusion became
so obvious
so empty
so meaningless
like I was there
watching, observing
the images
dancing by me
dancing with me
I struggled
I longed
I wished and
I let go
the illusion no longer
had power
nor meaning

it danced away
and with it
went too
my fantasies
my lies
my dependence
now, now am I free
free to dance
my own dance
free to make
my own music
free to sing
my own songs
free from the illusion
that was never real
free from the lesser
that was not me
never true
free from the dependence
that was not my own

– 4/05/1998

Whispers

Whispers from an angel
an angel
I had forgotten
not of her existence
but of her love
a love that changes
that distorts and
embraces the light
so I came to see
a light that filters
through the darkness
and whispers
whispers of hope
of quiet, of peace, of joy
a light that holds
a space where
love can grow
can be real again
can be nurtured
can be known
a light that reminds
me of my own light

a light that wants to
be turned up again
to allow others
to follow
as they choose
a light that is
made up of many
lights that touch
each other
and they all still whispering
come when it is right for you

– 4/21/1998

Pictures

Sleep dear one sleep
and in your sleep
dream of a time
once that you knew
and have forgotten

Let the pictures
color spaces in
your mind and
in your heart

Let the richness
of the beauty of
the magic dance
upon the canvas
of your mind
and of your heart

Like strokes
of light that
blend with each other
to touch
to form
a new world
a world that
enters into many
and all desire to see
but fear to look for

You have pictures
some are waiting
to be seen
not with our eyes
but with our
hearts and with
our souls

As your pictures
are envisioned
they will begin
to see their own world
and the pictures
that once were
lost will be
ever present in
our futures and
in our future's future
to lead us
into the places
we have forgotten
the places
we once have been

– 4/25/1998

Your Prison

I have not
been the
keeper of the prison
you find yourself in
I have not been
the one who locked
the door and
stayed inside
so no one could see
I do not hold
the keys to
that prison's door
nor do I want
to guard it
you create that
prison in where
you live
you lock the
door that will
not open
you hold the
keys to the
freedom you seek
open the door

– 4/26/1998

The Dunes

There was beauty here
unexplained beauty
found in the
curve of the dune
or swept together
in a mosaic of sand
there was sculpture
that reached into
the backdrop of blue
intermingled with brushes
of white wings that danced
across the sky
barren in the
images it portrayed
It spoke of the
beauty of loneliness
and of the essence
of finding portraits
of one's own self
in the corridors
of being alone
In its solitude
this place gave
voice to what
is beautiful without
speaking a word

– 4/27/1998

Finding the Way

Words so many words
almost screaming to
be laid down upon
the paper
as I wait for them
to come
they hesitate
then flow out
to me like
an unexpected storm
that moves through
and leaves as quietly
as it came
that leaves pieces of
nourishment along the way
and then disappears again
as quickly as it came
it wanted to rain
to rain in unending
torrents of words that
paint pictures
that capture feelings
that cry out to be heard
why is it never enough
for me

what is this drive
to know more
to see more
then my eyes can see
to hear
beyond what my ears
are in tune for
to touch those worlds
those deepest worlds
unknown to me
to feel the healing
rain wash over me
where we are always free
where I am free
free to dance
with the wind
and sail upon
the cresting waves
to dive deep
into the earth
in all its richness
in all its beauty
to be seen for
the first time
as I really am
let me find the way

− 4/28/1998

Another World

Sleep dear one sleep
and in your sleep
dream of a time
one that you knew
and have forgotten
color in the spaces
in your mind and
in your heart
let the richness
of the beauty
of the magic
dance upon the
canvas of your mind
and of your heart
like strokes of light
that blend with each touch
to form
a new world
a world that
enters into many worlds
and desires to seen
but fears to look for
yet you have pictures
that are waiting
to be seen
to be heard

not with eyes
but with hearts
not with tears
but in silence
for as you envision
your dreams
others will begin
to vision their own
in the pictures
that once were lost
will be ever present
in our future
and in our futures' future
to lead us
back to the place
we have forgotten
back to a memory of
where dreams live

– 4/29/1998

Win Your Heart

How do I give back the gift
a gift that now is so known
a space where light
and love come in
to make a place that is home

There isn't any reason
why love won't find a way
to our complicated hearts
where it can always stay

We only make excuses
and choices that confuse us
when love is held
confined and far away

How precious is the love
that always sets us free
how precious is the love
the time for you and me

The many ways I've left
with darker memories
I still remember now
that precious love to me

How do I win your heart
or will I ever know
that love is there
in part
to have a way to grow

– 8/23/1998

Now I Understand

I heard them say
feel the pain
go through the pain
seek out the pain
embrace the pain
let go but
I could not understand

I heard him say
this will end
you will find a way
you are strong enough
you are big enough
you are loved enough
and I did not understand

I heard them say
you need more love
you need to forgive
you can love again
there is a lesson here
you cannot stop now
and I did not understand

I heard him say
I love you
I see your pain
I know you are hurt
I believe and your strength
to love more
to forgive
and now I understand

– 4/02/1999

Of Our Children

They stood there
In the mist
like carvings
from an ancient time

They stood alone
but yet together
as they wait
for where it would
take them to

A place that
promises a different
life a better life
a learned way

They were so
expressionless as
they stood there
maybe waiting
and holding on
to the realness
within them

So afraid of
that which held
promises for their
futures were only
an allusion
that would cause
them to disappear
as many had before them

So they waited
In the mist
not knowing
what was to
become of their futures
yet they had to go

– 1/21/1999

You Are My Sons

You are my sons
sons I have chosen
sons I respect
you came to me
of your own choice
seeking as I too
to learn
to understand
to bring new meaning
to your lives and into mine

You are my sons
but also
you are sons
of this earth
sons of a world
that needs you
desires you to participate
to add value
to a unique need
in an individual place
and space that
you provide
for one or for many

– 5/19/1999

Ethan

This poem/free verse came to me just a few weeks after my first grandson Ethan Michael Smallie was born on May 5, 2004. Again as most of my writings or scribing filled the paper in 10 minutes or less. My second son was also born on May 5, 1973, Brent Michael Smallie. So we have much to celebrate on this historical day. The most significant is that of my son and my grandson entering our lives and our world on the fifth of May.

Little Man

Oh Little man with eyes so bright
Like sparking blue stars
That light up our night
And great big smiles
That stay and stay
and keep us laughing
All through the day.

Oh little man you are just right
for your big sister
To hold you tight
And hug your big cheeks
And want a bite
of your cute toes
And she just might.

Oh little man, your mom dad
Are so happy that you are here
To share your life
For it is clear
You are a blessing from above
That fills their hearts
With so much love.

So little man we celebrate
The fifth day you came
For it's so great
To have you in our family
Of love, and hope, and destiny
There are no words that really say
How God gives us for what we pray.

– California Grandpa, May 2004

Gwyneth

My first granddaughter was born in Marietta Georgia on 9/11/2001. Her birth was that morning just before the time of the horrific tragedy in New York. I experienced small piece of the pain of so many families and friends who lost their loved ones that day. The paradox was the joy I held in my heart of the birth of Gwyneth. I read later that many babies came into the world that same day. For me it was if those births were like many Angels who came into our world to try and heal some of the horrific pain for the loss so many were left with. That experience is what inspired this poem.

Her Name

Her name
it calls to you
her name it
speaks words
of light
of gentleness
of beauty.
She comes
to us
a blessing
to tiny yet
so infinite
so quiet yet
so eloquent.

She comes
to us
carrying a gift
a gift of herself
a gift to love
to treasure
to protect
a gift to hold
on our arms
a gift to lay
next to our hearts
so she may hear the
love inside us
that reaches out
to surround her.
Her name it is

Gwyneth

– California Grandpa, 9/11/2001

Chapter 4

Soul Whispers in the 2000s

Love flooded my life during this time from many directions. Love for myself, love of my spirituality, love for my sons and grandchildren and the love of the woman that is now my wife and eternal soulmate. Yes, there were struggles and battles and confusion but the light in my life became so brilliant at that time it was if darkness itself was blinded by it. The whispers from my soul reflected that over and over again, that love is a blessing from without and within.

Loving Hearts

Touching me
were so many
good hearts
hearts of passion
hearts of kindness
hearts of knowing
remember these hearts
for they are a piece
of your own
to see the light
in others
to see the light
in you

— 6/17/2001

Glimpses

Glimpses of the light
I see are only that
simply glimpses
yet they sustain me
through the darkest
of moments
even the remembrance
brings back a healing peace
sometimes I long for that light
I look so desperately
that there is no room
for the light to sit with me
so I then rest
and as I do the light
appears one more time
to hold and caress me
with its sinless beauty
only to be renewed
over and over again

– 9/03/2001

Her Eyes

Her eyes
they saw
through me
into my soul
I knew that
she knew
I did not
know why
I just knew
she saw a place
and me
a piece of me
I did not try
to hide
from her
she saw
my essence
my gift
my desire
to be
to be more
then I could be
she loved me
so deeply
so dearly

no one
nothing can
ever erase
that love
for it
now resides
in my heart
for her beauty
is now
my beauty
her gift
is now
my gift
her love has become
my love
I carry her
with me
each place I step
each person
I trust
I see with
her eyes
as I vision with
my own

the star I saw
in her eyes
I now see
and myself
shining its' radiant
light of love
of beauty
of peace
shining upon so
many lives
her eyes
her heart
still shines

– 9/18/2001

Life Again

You bring me
life again
capturing a place
in me
I had lost
so long ago

You make me
feel real again
like a star
that shines brightly
each night
upon the earth

You make me
feel known as
if you see
right inside me

You make me
feel life again
as if I could
soar into the heavens
eternally

– 8/11/2002

Our Love

I imagine you
at night
holding you
so tight
that I cannot
breathe
as my heart
my mind
are so filled
with the love
I hold for you
It is as if
I could burst
into a million
stars of light
spreading that love
our love
all over
the world
for others to be
nourished by

– 8/26/2002

Heartland

There was a time
where a river of love
flowed so deeply
in my life

There was a place
where no one could
ever touch or
move into

But you came down
a path I had never seen
and you crossed
a river that no
longer ever flowed
yes you moved into
the heartland of my soul

There was my heart
that waited patiently
for your love to come

There was a love
that awakened to
the words you spoke
and then I knew

But you came down
a path I had never seen
and you crossed
a river that no
longer ever flowed
yes you moved into
the heartland of my soul

And there is no
other love that
ever touched me
this way
and there is
no question
that my heart will
ever go our stay
for you have entered
the heartland
of my soul

– 8/27/2002

Let Me

Let me love
you
like you have
never been
loved
let me hold
you
like you have
never been
held
let me whisper
to you
of the beauty
I see
let me know
you
like you have
never been known

– 8/28/2002

I See You

When I look
up at the moon
I see you
arms wide open
embracing the love
as it melts
into your heart

When I look
up the moon
I see you
dancing on the
beams of starlight
that float across
the shadowed sky

When I look up
at the moon
I see you
eyes smiling
as only your
eyes can smile

When I look up
at the moon
I see your heart
so open
so tender
so strong
taking in and
giving out
the light
the love
it contains
When I look up
at the moon
I see your love
so radiant
so brilliant
it washes away
the fears we hold
and bathes us
in light of hope

– 8/29/2002

I Know You

I know you
from a time past
a time I
cannot remember
but I know
by the beating
of your heart
with mine
by the gaze
of your eyes
in mine
by the touch
of your hand
to mine
I know now
with every
breath I take
that our love
was born so
long ago
I know you

– 8/30/2002

A Thinking Heart

When my heart
starts thinking
I know it is
time to come back
to what is real
what is true
what is always
the love that
I hold for you

It is not about
thinking
it is not even about
feeling
it is about dreaming
dreaming of a love
that is so elusive
yet so inviting
so true that it
encompasses every part
of my world

It is not even about
feeling
it is about dreaming
dreaming of a love
that is so elusive
yet so inviting
so true that it
encompasses every part
of my world

Her love that holds
me tight at night
her love that remembers
when I forget
her love that just
will not let me go

When my heart
starts thinking
I always come back
to you

– 9/01/2002

The Dance

I found the one
who wants to
dance with me
to slide across sky
and into the stars
that encircle our hearts

I found the one
who wants to
dance with me
across the oceans
of time and
rest in my arms
and in my heart

When the dance
has ended
the music never stops
and the dance
never really ends

It only finds
a new rhythms
or a new step
we have never experienced

For we all dance
into the unknown
and back into hearts
of the ones who love us most

– 9/2/2002

A Brighter Day

Come lay with me
let me hear
the words you
whisper so softly
and yet with
such force

Let me touch the
beams of light
that penetrate
my inner being
and let me
hold the light
that washes
away all darkness

Let me see beyond
the worlds I know
and the feelings too
for a brighter day
is truly
up on the dawn

Let a day be filled
with so much hope that
it will burst
through every crevice
as it awaits
only for you
to receive the bounty
of a light that never ends

– 9/04/2002

She Called

She called
she called and
her voice connected
directly to my heart
it was not
so much the words
but the beauty
of her love
that spoke so
clearly to those
places that stood
so strong to
protect my heart
my soul
at the very center
of where my
love resided
and I knew
as I listened
with new
spaces which
had opened
that these words
we're true
they were real

and they healed
those places
those spaces
in an instant
with their love
with their compassion
with their tenderness

– 9/05/2002

Who Is She

Who is she
who is she
that makes
my heart sing

Who is she
that sees the
secret passages
to my heart

Who is she
who loves without
even asking why

Who is she
that senses the
pain that surrounds me

Who is she
that will never
leave my side

It is she
the one who
brings this light
who brings the
blessed ones to show
me the way

Who leads me
down a path
I have never seen

It is she
that I trust
with my love

It is she that
brings the light
that hold the vessels
which nurture me
and light my way

It is she

– 9/06/2002

Touching You

Touching you
I find strength
I never knew
love discovered
in a whisper or
a kiss
tender and warm
your love it
comes to me
it silently caresses
my face and
holds me passionately
in its arms and
speaks to me
beyond any language
I have ever known
it's words are
of beauty
of light
of happiness
of futures dreamed
of realities yet
untouched by anyone
or anywhere
in this world
or any others
that may exist

yet the knowing
of that love
is so real
that one only
need open
so slightly
a window in
their heart and
that love comes
flowing into
fill us up
so completely
so endlessly
the strength of
that love
will live on
forever into
our eternities

– 10/15/2002

I Will Fly

I will fly
to you
and hold you
deep, deep
within my heart
I will whisper
to you of
your beauty
and help you
remember who
you have
always been

I will sail
to you on
wings of golden
threads of love
and cocoon you
in a womb
of comfort
and of hope
in a safe place
where no one
can take your
beautiful love
away from

this world
or any of
your beauty

It surpasses
all this life
has ever known
and all the love
of past lives
you have left behind

This radiance
will forever
shine through
the pathways
of my soul
and yours
and open
doorways too
long closed
to that light
for your love
your beauty
can only
be seen
within the hearts
of those
who will open

to the mystery
of what it
holds so tenderly
so preciously
in its' arms

– 10/29/2002

Images

So many
beautiful images
I see
they flood
my mind
they lay softly
on my heart
they flow from
my tears

They cling fully
to every part
of me
they wait far
me at dawn
and they take
me to sleep
as the night
they come seeping in

They are pictures
of tenderness
a beauty
of hope
of joy
of a new
found freedom
that will
never cease

For those pictures
are from you
of your radiant love
that has entered
into me and
holds me
so tightly
when I no longer
can hold myself

The reminders of
my inner beauty
when clouds
of doubt
block my vision
yet whispers that
speak so powerfully
and yet so simply
you are loved
you are adored
you are my love

– 12/04/2002

Your Love

Your love
is right there
in my face
calling me
to take a stand
seeing me
in distant lands
visioning me
with eyes unseen
teaching me
of who I've been

your love
is right there
in my heart
teaching me
I am not alone
leading me
to find my home
touching me
with quiet love
helping me
to look above

Your love
 is right there
in my being
embracing me
in an image new
finding me
in worlds more true
leaving me
beside still waters
transporting me
to sacred quarters
never failing
or digressing
your love
is like an angel's blessing

– 4/21/2003

Since You

I was standing all alone
without a place to call my home
till you, till you came into my life

I was waiting outside your door
dreaming of a life with more
and you, yes you walked into my life

Now I hear a voice
that paints another choice
the choice for loving you
the gift of loving you

And those who've heard that voice
we'll stand with you and me
they'll sing to every mountain top
and the whisper to every tree

Now God stands in our hearts
and you stand next to mine
the love that seemed so distant then
that touches your soul
that touches mine
since you, since you came into my life

– 8/3/2003

Reflections in Monterey

From Granite City to Monterey
seems like a short distance to get to play
on a classic stage were Hendrix
performed and etched the burned symbols
of the intensity of his music
for others to be inspired
Jimi to be reincarnated once again
in the rhythms, riffs, and stretches of each string

Yet the roads to this stage are many
roads that no longer exist
but where memories still wait
through avenues of change
of pain
of one more successful gig
or maybe one more dissonant performance
for those who really can't hear the music

In my mind
in my heart one stands out
next to yet above all the rest
for his youthful enthusiasm and
is ever present smile light up this stage
with a simple confidence and yet
complex knowledge and experience
of what and how he plays so well
that once child
now man
from Granite City

– 10/03/2008

Two Hearts

One then two hearts beating
beating as one
reaching out
for the rhythm
for each other to feel
to touch
that loving beat again
and again
forever united in an
unexplained union
of mystery of love

Her love that never departs
even when those two hearts
appear alone for awhile
that beat of unending love
goes on and on
as a gift to each other

Even in brief moments
when the rhythm is
not in sync
there is no gift greater
then that of such
a soulful love

That love as
that beat goes on
reaching out to retouch
to regain that desire
for harmony
two lovers whose hearts
that long to be one

– 12/24/2008

Cleansed

Little tiny raindrops
fall in cleanse
our earth
and cleanse
our hearts

lighting sparks
the sky above
and touches
our spirits
with sacred love

thunder invites
the earth to
tremble and awaken
our souls with
dreams of splendor
I with you and
you with me
held in love eternally
we rest

– 11/27/2009

On That Day

On that day you were born
a sweet tenderness
flowed into this world
and it reached out to
ignite four tiny stars
that had been waiting
so long for your touch
and the four stars came
from the heavens to be
be held in your tenderness
surrounded by your light

The first one came
blazing to you
like a dazzling comet,
then two more sliding
through the skies like
too soft and gentle doves,
and the fourth came rolling
into you as if he were a
ball of light so full of laughter
they all rested secure in
your heart, safe in your arms,
help tenderly in your soul

On the day they were born
the heavens became a new place
a safe and loving home for all
who were touched
by your brilliant light
and special love

There are others who still
patiently await for you
to more fully see the light

There is one who has
already been sparked by
your bountiful love and
holds that love as an
exquisite and precious gift

On the day you were born
so many are thankful

– 5/16/2010

Chapter 5

Soul Music

There was a brief time when my soul began to speak to me in a musical structure with verse, chorus and bridge. The first song, The Child Left In Between, is highlighted at the beginning of this chapter. It was the most distinct and clear voice I had ever heard. The strength and insistence of this song finally awakened me to the fact that all of these pictures in words were God speaking through my soul. It was and is a blessing immeasurable to hear such a voice from within and realize that God is always close at hand.

My First Song

The inspiration for THE CHILD LEFT IN BETWEEN came to me from an experience while traveling on a business trip. I had missed a flight connection in Phoenix and had to go through Las Vegas. That meant I was not going to get back home to Fresno until after 2 a.m. I was upset, angry, and feeling sorry for myself. Sitting in the airport I noticed a little girl sitting with a man who was very large in stature. She was probably eight or nine years old. They were sitting there not saying much. I had the feeling it was her father and she was flying back to be with her mother. It felt like it was a common scene from a movie for a child whose parents were separated are divorced.

I stepped onto the plane and set down in the first row. Minutes later the little girl boarded the plane. Her hair and eyes reminded me of my granddaughter. The flight attendant ask if the little girl could sit next to me. Tears were streaming down her face. I, of course, said yes. I asked her if she was afraid of flying and what her name was. She said she was not afraid yet I felt her deep sadness. Before the plane even lifted from the runway she laid her little head on my shoulder and fell fast asleep. Every time there was even a little bump should she would nuzzle closer to me and fall off to sleep again.

A few months later I was flying from Fresno back through Las Vegas. The memory of that frightened and sad little girl came rushing back to me. As the plane lifted from the ground there were words in the form of a song came popping into my consciousness. I did not have a pen our paper so I grabbed a highlighter marker and tore out a page from a magazine and began to write. All of these words came to me in less than 20 minutes. When the seatbelt sign went off, I raced from the plane and found a pen and transposed those faint yellow highlighter words, line by line, onto paper.

That was the first time words ever came to me in the form of a song. The lyrics came in two verses, a chorus, and a bridge. No music just distinct and explicit words.

The song, A Child Left in Between, to me are lyrics about children of separation or divorce or of those who have been abused in some way. In my experience it has not been a topic or lyric that has been addressed much in the world of music. Songs talk about breakups and heartaches of men and women. We have not seemed to find the words to express the separation the children feel in splitting their time and love between two homes or of parents they are afraid to be with. They are truly the children that are left in between.

Many times, as my two sons experienced my own divorce, I was so busy dealing with our own emotions that I forget the most important people to love through that crisis was my children. This song challenged me to be more aware and I hope it will challenge other parents as well. Those who were once committed to each other must find a path of love in raising their children. A path with a commitment greater than just themselves but even greater for their children left in between.

The Child Left in Between

VERSE 1:

Her head lay on my shoulder
as the plane lifted from the ground
she nuzzled close next to me
as a tear came trickling down
her brown eyes closed so tightly
as if no one were around
she slept restlessly, yet silent
as we flew towards her home
the loss she'd left behind her
were now in dreams so still untold
in a world yet undiscovered
in a place she did not know.

VERSE 2:

She didn't know quite what to feel
as he sat there in that chair
his silence was so deafening
he did not seem to care
no smile left there upon his face
she looked closely for a sign

for the love he once held sacredly
seemed gone or far away
she was being sent back one more time
with only loneliness to face
to a home that really was no home
only an empty place to stay.

CHORUS:

She is the one
the one we see so many times
she is the child
yes, the one who's left behind
by a mom and dad
that just can't seem to see
a love that's bigger
than they both care to be
so the child they have
the one there in-between
between the love she's lost
and the love she's never seen.

BRIDGE:

We can't find out all the answers
to questions we don't know
for the love a mom and dad once held
can be melted like the snow
but we can give our children
who are left there in-between
a path of light and grace and love
so they can always see.

REPEAT CHORUS

Captured All My Love

– 5/01/2005

I was just fine alone
no need to go home
to anyone or anything
for the rest of my life
I knew I would be alright
with my heart I had no shame
but then you came along
your love was so strong
I couldn't stop to take a breath
you came into my heart
I didn't know where to start
I only knew what was left.

Now you've captured all my love
and you won't let it go
no matter where that I start
you're always there I know
I can't resist your sweet touch
there is just so much
a man can ever take
so I welcome your love
I thank the lord above
that love makes no mistakes.

Now that door has opened up
there's no way I can shut
your love out of my mind
you can tell by all the tears
that I have left each and every fear
so many miles behind
I just long for the day
when the words that I say
comfort you and then
all the love that you have
given me will be recaptured
in your heart once again.

–

Hear the Music

– 8/05/2005

Its' like this
it comes to me
I don't know from where
it takes by pen
and leads me there
the words are soft
or sometimes hard
but it comes to me
sometimes in part
to tune me out to
so I can listen again
to those old messages that always spin
inside my head or inside my heart
and try to end the song I start
but I won't let them
because I know
there is only one place I need to go.

To hear the music
the words sung out loud
that you can hear them
no matter what surrounds
your day
your life
your family
that soothing music
the kind that sets you free
to dance to live
in such a way
That sweet sweet music
brings you a brand new day.

Its seems so simple
just to let it go
but then life grabs you
and you know
you can't be happy
there is so much to bear
you struggle on and
fall into despair
then something happens
you just can't explain
you hear the music
and live starts once again.

To hear the music
the words sung out loud
that you can hear them
no matter what surrounds
your day
your life
your family
that soothing music
the kind that sets you free
to dance to live
in such a way
That sweet sweet music
brings you a brand new day.

–

He's Always Been Here

– 10/03/2005

I heard my grandma say
when my grandpa passed away
he's not coming back I know
it's like he's never been
in the moments of my life
now all stand still without an end
he's left me all alone
it feels just like a sin
I know not where he's gone
he's not coming back again.

It saddened me that day
to hear my grandma say
those words that were so cold
of a man she'd loved and known
he had knocked upon her door
and he'd welcomed her right in
to a life so full of light
and a love that would not end.

I finally said to her
with tears that filled my eyes
he's always been here
right next to you
he's always been here
with a love that is so true
so won't you sense him
his heart is clear and true
he's reaching out his hand now
he's always been here
right next to you.

He held her hand one last time that day
and he's never let it go
and although he's passed away
he still holds her close I know
and she's finally realized
as I've seen it in her eyes
he has never left her side
or gone far from her heart
and although he's left this earth
they have never been apart.
after years she left this earth
not knowing where he had been
but she holds his hand today
in a new life without end.

They're not coming back I know
but it's like they've always been
in the moments of moments
of my life
they all stand here
without end
they've left everything that was
no it's surely not a sin
they've moved on
I know exactly where
they're not coming
back again.

It Couldn't Happen

– 5/25/05

It couldn't happen without her
the love she smiles
the love she breathes
right into my very heart
and it reignites my dream
it couldn't happen without her
the way she's loved me from the start
it never happened until she
played the leading part.
I have spent some forty years
holding onto an old dream
it's come and gone just like the wind
it was impossible it seemed
I found no other way to live
but I gave life all I had
yet it never seemed enough
it was too hard to believe.
We went to Nashville one weekend
just to celebrate the days
when we were born
into this world
it didn't seem that far away
we sat and listened to the songs
that the masters writers write
and as the tears streamed
down my face

she squeezed my hand so tight
the words she spoke I'll never forget
as she whispered in my ear
you know I think the time is right
for you to write those songs you hear.

I'm still amazed each day I sit
and listen to the lyrics that come and go
they play inside my grateful heart
they sing inside my thankful soul
the beat a rhythm that won't stop
for now it's the only way I know
to write the dreams she helped me see
and hear the words that capture me
It couldn't happen without her
the way she loved me from the start
it never happened
until she played
the leading part.

Lost All the Light

— 5/02/05

You're going out of your mind
trying hard to find
a way that you can win
you don't know how I feel
all your cruel words do reveal
is the hurt down deep inside
I can no longer take
the abuse that's your mistake
for something that is true
you have closed heart and mind
and I don't have the time
for the love that it would take.

You have lost all the light
that once was in your eyes
your pain is way too big
and there's no compromise
for the hate deep inside
that you knew was bound to win
you know no other way
but to hear people say
they failed you once again
you've walked out of your life
and there just seems no way
to bring you back again.

You've found out what its' like
to live the rest of your life
living with the pain
and there's no other way
no matter what I say
that it will ever end
you have locked yourself uptight
and no one can make it right
there's no love anyone can send
for you've lost all your light
the darkness is your friend

Lucky in Love

— 6/03/05

How many guys get this lucky
you know what I mean
it's just oh so good
you just can't believe
how good it is
and great it will be
once again to get lucky
well I'm sure you must see
that my world turns around
I'm lost in that place
there is no other feeling
on this earth that takes place
like loving my lady
you know what I mean
cause I'm lucky in love
it's more than it seems.

I'm lucky in love
there is no place I'd be
because of her love
it has me so free
to be who I am
for now I so see
that I'm lucky in love
and it's her that's made me

You might think that this song
is about how you manipulate love
and try to make it right
but it's so much more than that
it's about her eyes and
about her kiss
it's about all the things
you will miss
if you don't see love
as it truly is
it's about the words
inside your head
that just won't stop
until they are said
in the dream you picture
your life with her can be.
when you lucky in love

Paradise

– 5/18/05

Just twenty acres at the river's edge
surrounded by rich fields
of green and brown
and sometimes gold
that never seemed to end
the California sun
shines down each day
to bless our humble home
it's the place I always want to stay
and don't ever want to leave

I call it paradise
I never want to leave
I know its paradise
it's in my heart you see
I'd find no other place
that leads me to this door
I call it paradise
it's the place that fills my soul

Why do I always have to go
it shouldn't be that way
when you're all wrapped up
in so much love
don't you always want to stay
this place has captured me I know
I won't ever go away
for when your life is filled with paradise
don't you always want to stay

My heart aches so each time I leave
it just knows no other way
for there's so much beauty here I see
and it goes on day to day
I won't ever find another place
just to rest my weary soul
for this place that I call paradise
is the place I've always known

I call it paradise
I never want to leave
I know its paradise
it's in my heart you see
I'll find no other place
that leads me to this door
I say it paradise
it's a place that fills my soul.

Reflections

– 5/23/05

Reflections of a place I've been
yet I know it's not the same
for a life that's filled with so much joy
never wants to know the pain
how I long to have my whole self back
not to suffer or be away
for my family needs me and I know
yes it is time for me to pray.

Oh dear God will you please look down on me
while you lift me up
for the love I have upon this earth
is so big you can't disrupt
all there is and all I've lived to be
it just scares me deep inside
for I know you have to plainly see
it's not time for me to die.

When the doctors told me the bad news
I asked the scene to be replayed
it might be right for someone else I said
but for me there's just no way
for my life just has no room for this
I choose living everyday
if this has to be the hand I'm dealt
then it's time for me to pray.

Now I lived a life with so much pride
that will never go away
for my friends all stand right by my side
and I always here them say
you're a good man and no matter what
we're all with you all the way
for a man who's loved as much as you
we just know you've got to stay
and if God will listen one more time
then it's time for us to pray.
oh dear God will you please look down on him
while you lift him up
for the life he's lived upon this earth
is so big you surely can't disrupt
all he is and all he wants to be
it would hurt us deep inside
for we know You have to plainly see
it's not time for him to die
for we know You have to plainly see
it's not time for him to die.

Seeing Her Seeing Me

– 6/3/05

She sat down next to me
in this little Mexican bar you see
where the beers are expensive
but the chips and salsa were free
and she asked me without any hesitation
what's wrong with you
you don't seem the same
it was all I could do
to hold back the tears
as I tried to explain
how I'd lost all those years
to one that I thought
I had always known
but her eyes looked at me
and her love still showing
as she reached out a hand
in a moment or two
she wiped off the tears
of a woman I knew.

Seeing her seeing me
in those eyes
I'd never seen
they were eyes
with so much love
no one could ever doubt
what she's made of
for her heart was oh so free
and her eyes spoke words to me
that I cannot quite explain
yet her love it still remains
in my heart
it touches me
her eyes are seeing me.

The beers kept on flowing
and the words never stopped
as we shared our life's stories
from the bottom to the top
it seemed we had known
a time and a place
where our lives had once met
in a life and a space
we had seemed to forget
I know it sounds crazy
but we'd both tell you so
as we walked out from that bar
and met another time down the road.

The next time we met
it was over a year
our lives had both changed
but the love was still clear
it was always unspoken
yet apparent to us
we had met for a reason
we both had to trust
and remembered a time
when we wanted out souls
to live out a love
yet it couldn't be so
so we moved on alone
but now was the time
to hear to our hearts say
this love is all ours
it is now here to stay.

Song in His Soul

– 5/30/05

He told me when he as just ten years old
dad I've got to play, it's in my soul
and so the music came and grew
but so did he and before I knew
he was a bass player in band to band
sometimes the crowd would give him a hand
then there were times they were silent
but he would still stand
with that glowing smile upon his face
to the beat of the band
and the rhythm of his bass
it was awesome man

There were times that were dark
as his love progressed
and he almost died
and put his dreams to rest
but somehow through all the drugs and pain
he could still hear his soul
yes it called him by name
it would never release him or let him go
he had something to say
so he kept on believing
and still knows till this day.

Son you've got a gift to give
don't you know you have
a song to live
there is no one here to take your place
so play it with so much soul and grace
that you knew some twenty years ago
cause by my side you told me so
you said dad I've got a song to play
its' inside my soul, won't go away
I don't know why the music holds me so
but it's a song that sings inside my soul.

Now his path still leads him many ways
but he keeps on playing everyday
for his wife, and kids and family
they see it in his heart
and although they feel
the times they miss when he's away
they still hear his music
and they each say.

Its' inside his soul, won't go away
he doesn't know
why the music holds him so
but it's inside his soul
won't go away.
it's in his soul
will never go away.

Southern Lovin

– 5/24/05

I love the South
where they call you honey
and it makes no difference
how much money you spend
or what you look like
or what you do
sometimes its sweetie
and sometimes it's darlin
and the words like that
they just keep coming
and you walk outside
just like you are brand new.

It's all about that Southern lovin
there's no place on earth
that's this much like heaven
when you walk through those bar doors
and the place is all about you
so take it all in
don't make no mistakes
of waiting on something
it' never too late
to live the life you've
always wanted to.

Southern that Southern lovin
it holds you tight
never lets you down
lovin that Southern lovin
you can't find it in any other town
so breathe it, live it
eat it, be it
there's enough to go around
lovin that Southern lovin
it never let's you down.

Bridge:

When you walk into those honkeytonks
those country songs just grab your heart
and you don't know whether to dance or sip a few
while you listen to those old sad songs
or the ones about love that are so strong
that make you cry and remind you
you've been there too.

Wake Up and Listen

– 6/24/05

There's a lot of you here
she said as a whisper
as she walked out the door
there's a lot of you here
but I'll tell you mister
I'm not one of those things you own
there's a lot more to me
than just being fooled with
and I've got more pride than to stay
with a man who must think
that love it a toy
that I'm here just for the play.

But you have no power
to do what you do
I'm sorry your life
is so hurtful to you
but I can't be staying
with someone not true
to the love life has given
without any price
so here's something darling
please take my advice.

Wake up and listen
before it's too late
this world around you
is more than just a date
of one night stands
and games you play
so wake up and listen
before it's too late.

You're more than you think
you're more than you do
you keep a real women
from really loving you
it's time that you stop
and re-evaluate
what you think is love
what you say is fate
so I'll try to tell you
just one more this time
won't you please listen
and take my advice.

Wake up and listen
before it's too late
this world around you
is more than just a date
of one night stands
and games you play
so wake up and listen
before it's too late.

Welcome to My Dreams

– 4/29/05

Welcome to my life she said
you're welcome to my dreams
you don't know how hard it's been
to find out what it means
to be more than an after thought
or more than something seems
to have more than the life I've led
you're welcome to my dreams.

It was all I had to give
seemed it never was enough
found myself without the love
I'd been dreaming of
didn't know there was a chance
for a girl like me
I wanted more than just romance
to be more than I could be.
four kids I loved with all my heart
there seemed no room for more
but when he walked into my life
I'm the one he now adores.

Life has taken such a turn
it's all I dreamed I'd have
a man who so much honors me
and loves me as I am
this love we have will never end
it always has to be
cause we are blessed with so much more
than most lives ever see
cause we are blessed with so much more
than most lives ever see.

Epilogue

My hope is that there are more chapters still to be written in my life. I pray there are many years and vibrant and meaningful words that will continue to appear in both my unconscious and conscious worlds. In fact, writing this book is actually one of them. As I have been stuck on the mechanics of constructing this book I again began to realize that all I had to do was let go and let my soul do the talking. So one more time I have a chance to learn and relearn, to listen and listen again to those shouts and whispers from my soul.

Forever

Forever yours
forever mine
held together
in a time
so close and too
so very real
enclosed by
hearts that
only feel
the eternal beat
of loving hope
of times remembered
of words not spoke
not only sighs
and breathless love
but streams of love
that flow like torrents
of raining hearts
from up above
where time stands still
in all that love
of hearts so touched
of love so reached
we stand together
as two united
with hearts in hand
with love replenished
our hearts, our love
will never finish.

– 2/14/2017